Dedicated to those who have come, and gone, before us.
May you continue to illuminate us along the paths of life...

This book is a curated offering in honor of servitude, and to the edifice of this country. May God bless America in all of her laudable undertakings, as they are what will allow for her to prosper and endure.

All proceeds go to:

The Pets for vets foundation
The Tough mudder litter O course to sponsor vets
The Franklin project

About the Author:

Most of the pillars and mentors in my life have served this country, whether in office or in uniform. I of my own free will and accord, accepted the same honor of servitude. This service is directed to and for a country of possibilities that allow for the inherent good of man to shine through unknown darkness. This unknown darkness needs exploring and probing at all times in order to make the unknown, the known.

There are things that lie within the dark, good and bad. We must shed light into dark corners to afford for a better understanding of positioning and possibilities of movement. There are certain people who are tapped to do such tasks and can operate in the light as well as the dark with surgical precision. I honor their ambiguity, diligence and service.

While serving this country I fell deeper in love with the ideals of the country that birthed us, and the world that birthed her, much like loving your parents, even more so for having birthed you, your brother and or sister. The love I have for my country and siblings civilian and veteran alike ha, grown and cultured with time and experience.

We have all lost friends and family here in this country and abroad. They fought and died for what this country could be, and is, at its best. Our forefathers, family and friends gave their lives to service of an ideal of our country. For that cause there is no option other than our Great Nation to be bettered by the effects of their service.

Black the color of all pupils
Black the complete absorption of light
Black the color of the unknown which contains the known

There has been a dueling thought process surrounding the ideologies of how people and we as central pangean beings (Lucy-Darwin) identify ourselves and articulate that identity to other distinguishing factors of the human race. There is irrefutable science that states that the origin of man has come from Africa. Yet as Afrocentric Americans (yes this encompasses white european americans as well, based on scientific discoveries)we have not been able to accept and connect our direct path to origins outside of complection. The african culture was absolved and or diluted and and its remnant were to be absorbed by the conquering western cultures.

Harkening back to a time when Americans started publicly vocalizing and demonstrating their perspective, they began to groan, toss and turn in their spiritual slumber. They were being subjugated and treated as secondary citizens, which inherently disregarded the reality of their original status as original man. Movements such as civil rights touted slogans such as "I am a Man" with no regard to who the person making that statement was talking to. There is also a point That the slogan does not allow for the person stating it, to profess their knowledge of themselves, already knowing who or what they are. I am a man, vs "I know I am a man".

The first states that I would desire for you and I to recognize what and who I am. The latter states that regardless of what your perspective may be in regards to my stature I have secured and I am secure in the knowledge that I am a man, and it is up to you, the unbeliever of that to catch up with that fact. The same go for movements to date such as "No Justice No Peace" vs "Justice is Peace". The simplicity of the difference in semantics and its implications may seem minuscule yet the results are staggering.

It is the equivalent to moving a flashlight that is on the floor. The actual movement of the light may be small but the area that the light covers changes drastically with its small movement. A few enlightened words (the flashlight) uttered by millions (the echo chamber of marches, demonstrations and social media) equal the span and range of the flashlight. The true question is the depth and strength of the light after it reaches its subject and duration and power of its batteries.

These movements and slogans have changed altered and morphed over the following generations. In today's society we have slogans such as black lives matter. These moments have been undermined by their inception due to their inability to recognize the flashlight scenario in regards to the movements identity and the vocabulary it utilizes. To identify your movement synonymously with a name that allows for the misinterpretation and or misrepresentation of its values and morals to allows for that misdirection to resonate or echo it effectively ineffective, through time.

By naming the movement black lives matter then chanting black lives matter those who support and or employ either idea or agenda force themselves to be identified with the vilification of the movement. This is due to the small crack or chink in the movement's/slogans due to semantic misunderstanding which then leads to misinterpretation and the miscommunication of purpose. Yet the intention/spirit of the slogan is lost under the compounded dogma and politicized agendas and semantic.

Now we may proceed with a more keen idea on how to realize, verbalize and express the movements of the past and from them taking the positives, and knowledge and apply it to the movements that will subsequently follow. The black lives matter movement falls prey to the same issues as the "I am a man" pitch from the 60's. The movement would have had a better chance at gauging depth, and casting a wider net in relation to catching/getting/securing the basic understanding and thought process of its participants and observers, if it insinuated and verbalized its purpose more articulately. I.e. "Black lives matter to me"! The addition of to me allows for the participant and observer to have some stake in the slogan and the movement while still allowing both to maintain some autonomy.

These semantics are a necessity in its judgment, understanding or condemnation (vilification). This has a plethora of meaning a protester could utter the words with the intention that the deaths by the hands of police once committed unjustly go to the heart of what the slogan stands for, yet a privatized prison owner could utter the same words and his intention could be completely nefarious. The addition of the word to me also allows for the veil of misdirection to be lifted, revealing intention. This movement and its predecessors have been the grogginess of a narcoleptic country, world and people, as it slowly awakens to a new day (era/age) before its next exhaustive slumber.

As our eyes open to a whole new world, they are forced to slowly focus for the appropriate reception of light and its varying colors. This reigns true for the the initial eye opening women's and civil rights movements or children's rights near the turn of the century. It is now time for another critical blink as the country and world awakens and clears the crusted tears from its eyes. That blink makes unjust deaths, corrupt government officials, and ill intentioned government or the basic disregarded necessities of the lower echelons of the caste system, resulting in the festering of maoism.

The caste system which we have built our capitalist democracy on top of and around. This model has been formed and emulated by many successful societies i.e. India, all of Europe, Asia and then transplanted to the west by colonialism which is synonymous with colonization. With the foundation of the Red the White and the Blue it required that the caste system be the spine to support its future extremities and appendages .

In vedic practice there was a need for your born echelon to be filled and maintained throughout your life, locking into this system/experiment a lower classes of people based off of race(color) vs the actual value of each individual and their merits. The initial experiment of America never accounted for the future generations of immigrant and slave cultures to realize that they were implanted into the system, and that they had the inalienable rights to maneuver within it based on its historic and significant ideologies.

The American experiment or experience allows for the lower echelons of the system to be bolstered by immigrants and those looking to transcend themselves from a smaller caste system of their own social relation into a caste system of the largest scale which offers a larger probability of growth, America.

This growth and idea of transcending class or echelon of caste, is the passionate identity, and symbolic idea of the American dream. As with any multifaceted experience the American experiment today there are varying degrees of thought, emotion and action, on all levels of class/caste. Think if America were a thermometer with those who fully realize its systems on one end are not able to realize those on the other, there is no difference in the relativity of what is cold or hot because it is all temperate on the thermometer.

If you are at the bottom of the 99 percent or the top 1 percent you are both still fully living out the American dream. That inequality of experience allows for you to have an unequally equal unilateral experience with those who do not share that same perspective or have not been affected in the same degree in which you may have been.

With the classes/caste echelons, again referencing the thermometer analogy, we have been able to group or clump together overarching relative ideals and or values cold, cool, warm or hot. This is imbued in the tea party movement, black lives matter, super pacs and grass root movements. It takes a significant number of people to change what each class or caste echelon looks like yet it takes only one individual to be the polarizing degree between what is a warm 79 degrees to what is a hot 80 degrees and that itself can be relative to orientation.

As a species we are centered around social interaction. as we made the transition from hunter gatherers to occupying and agriculture we have not lost our primary purpose of life, the perpetuation of ourselves. whomever we identify ourselves as - your tribe from the hunter gatherer time reference , class and caste echelons of Eurasian and western cultures, or people as a species in relation to our place in our macro universe. Our view, sight and focus become sharper with every passing day.

That identity changes once it/you is adopted by the western culture. Western culture purposely disregards the allowance of self sole identification to its any echelon, by altering and priming them once they take part in its western culture. Ie- you are no longer India but Indian American you are no longer African rather African American etc. This naturalization or super imposed identity adds another galvanizing layer to the American experiment and experience.

This layering effect locks in a mindset or points of reference as to the polarizing origins of where the person receiving the identity has come from,insinuating movement, to who they are viewed as now, and how they and their future lineage and related cultures have the probability of being viewed/critiqued/judged.It is up to you, whoever you identify with, your class(tribe), caste echelon and superimposed identity to alter the status quo (be that degree that is a significant positive distinction on the thermometer from one temperature feeling to the next).

It takes a village or villages were the keystone in transitioning from hunter gatherer tribes to the city states we now live in Today. There must be realization of where the standard was, ie: Lucky to Mansa Musa, all other people and color factions that follow were evolutions from the evolving original civilizations before east-western (Persian,Greek,Roman) culture grew large enough to engulf them. The expectation of movement should be and must be initiated and met every varying level and throughout all classes/caste levels and factions. You're formation of a new tribe or aspiration to form with one with all of it's/ your implied identities. Each identity has an ability to individually maneuver in different areas/classes/caste level/faction of the American experiment experience are the catalyst for change.

Dating, marrying and divorcing, within and outside of one's race has allows the realization that the cultural differences we experience are a part of what the American dream is on all echelons. It dilutes and simultaneously concentrates all portions of the experience creating more possibilities/opportunity of difference within the polarity.

America was built on the caste system with the possibility of the four versions of Aristotelian government (democracy-ran by the people for the people, oligarchy-ran by those who own and or have access to a majority of property and resource, aristocracy- ran by those who are educated and have embodied and embolden institutions, monarchy- ran by one man or bloodline residing over all others) these forms were to be draped upon caste /class systems. For America to state that social mobility is the "American dream" within its borders is for it to first recognize that outside of its borders there is a restriction of the mobility it intrinsically boast.

For america to state that it allows for class or upward mobility it inherently recognizes that mobility is restricted in many other geographical locations, that too, like america harken back to a caste/class system, and which are draped on one of the four forms of government which may not be democracy. Class or caste draws upon the mindset of sharing specific socio economic associations among others in your class or caste level, and residing in them from birth to old age.

It can be said that what we all share is better because we all share it, but the opposite can be also stated that what is rarer is more coveted because it is only possessed by few. Yet it takes both to comprise and co-create the other. There will innately be an inequality in anything shared (money, suffrage, education) until after it is shared, yet it is who notices the inequality and how they choose to view the cause and effect of that inequality that matters more.

This divide is further perpetuated as we dissect things into parts since breaking them down produces a larger number than what it was before, the individual portions equaling the sum total. The further we categorize people based upon any thing that can be humanly viewed ie complexion, money, food, and the resource or resources the more we do them service of bringing them to equality through inequality, appreciating each intricate individual aspect for what it is in relation to the whole. The visual form of this is a pie or bar chart, the entire chart shows the range of one thing that is comprised of many others that are measured against itself and each other in relation to the whole. The same goes for those residing in the same country along with their resources.

~ To blind a one eyed man inflicts more injury

than blinding a man with two eyes.

Either way both are forced to heightened senses.

Red the color of passion
Red the color of love and hate
Red tape the distance between caste/class levels

-Seeing Red-

I have had family, friends and ancestors live and die in and for this country. I simply assume that the reader can state the same for their own family, friends and ancestors. With this base understanding we will continue to galvanize the foundations for the rest of this reading.

As a millennial, I was born and raised in this country and I am the fifth generation (as far as I know) of my family that has lived in this country with two of the five generations being under colonial enslavement. My forefathers the have lived and died here in america over the past five generations if not more. I as a third generation a brown/black American man who has served his country during a period of war as a medic.

After experiencing first hand the pain and startling results of dogma agendas. I come home to a tattered country feeling the echos and groans of the prior generations as we debate the fabric of our Great Nation down to the minutsia of its fibers. Witnessing engagements that aristotelian concepts would call separatism. We the people, are seeing more red tape of division compounding the tacky adhesiveness of arcane thinking and policy, at a time when we desire to stick together the most

-Shout to MY Rednecks-

Rednecks received their name sake from working outside in open fields that were worked on and by slaves, servants, some indentured and sharecroppers. They were the class of laborers that sought the opportunity to ease and alleviate the strain of the class they were in, as well as aspire toward the possibility of upward mobility. They were the caucasian americans that would lovingly call their roots the country, "stix", "boonie's", or "backwoods". These were also the class of laborers that were selected as a "buffer zone" to be rolled into a fold to bolster the ranks of anglo saxon caucasians american society.

These sturdy americans were looked at initially by complexion, language and lineage to ascertain and justify certain portions of their socioeconomic status. They were regarded as though there was no distinction between them and other races including, Italians, Irish, Afro-centric Americans (Blacks), Asian and people of Hispanic/Latino descent. It was not until the baby boomer era that the "nuclear family and a cadillac" (the American dream) was possible to the "everyday American". During the times of immigration swells in america from the Irish, Italian, and Asiatic arrivals those who felt as though their country was slipping away to immigrants hid behind the guise of nationalism (not to be confused with Patriotism) to propel national idea of separatism. Separatism allows for subjective discrimination, rather than unbiased objective discernment.

By attempting to further fortify position within America and by creating a larger subjective or emotional based ideological buffer created by the possibility of access and inclusiveness created zone of cover and concealment using the everyday American. Realizing that the majority of the Anglo Saxon camouflage came from completion and language dialect which is largely based on geographic location, it also lent itself to spiritual belief.

Often throughout time it has been warped and fine tuned to enroll religion into the defining of its discriminatory factors along with color and geographic location. This has instigating and incited ignorance, fear mongering and anger in order to maneuver, pacify, subjugate or subdue. There is roughly 325 million people in the united states who are subject to subliminal deviciness. It is understandable why some americans are seeing red as they attempt to cut through the minutia compounding levels of red tape while aspiring for the American dream.

~Tackiness: Being out of date, and or stuck,
leaving behind undesired residue.

White a colorless coloring agent
White the color devoid of color pigment or hue
White color of peace

-WHITE FLAG TAG- You're it...

In the previous pages we have covered how America became the supposed "white" America, we know there is no such thing as a white america now knowing that most of its inhabitants from its very inception were immigrants of ranging complexion. We now arrive at a place where we have recognized individual races and their pigmentation in peripheral realms in example, geographic locations, language and spiritual proclivities and opinions of belief. Now we shall take a look into the discourses between the people of America through the usage of government, political (rhetoric which appeals to the subjective opinion of the objective), classes/caste level.

To highlight these points I will recall the words of a President of the United States. His daughter spoke these words to a major news organization, "My dad and I get out of our car(that was chauffeured) and we walk past a homeless man out front of OUR building, my dad points at the desolate man and tells me to take a good look at him (the homeless man), he has more money than me.

This relative distortion is also portion of the mentality of America that has been embedded in it since its inception. From the wars based on taxation to those of ownership of people being used as slaves, it's been a story of relative perseverance via relative persecution. This is echoed at every level within our society. From section 8 housing, to trumped up skyscrapers in our nation's cities. Most feel as though they were given a raw deal, not taking into account how relative "raw" here in America may be not be to them. To look at what is raw in other places in the world would mean to rely on the same sustenance as the person in comparison.

This is a significant point that is looked at in Maoism which takes the perspective of the lower level of the caste system and allows them to see that they do not have the numbers of the people on their side to assist in fulfilling their needs(which is resources/money rather the people who own them). Hence the movements like occupy wall street and the point argument of the 99 percent.

These movements undertake the mindset that, if there is a perception that things can be better, then we should all work to assist in making it so. Those who maintain their usage of the white flag mentality, as that President did with his daughter are the other side to that coin, they peacefully surrender to a mentality falls in line with a victim of capitalism globalization and that of a miser.

Free enterprise allows all who have the resources (who you know) and who desire to use it to over time become agile in relation to acquiring additional resources, money, and wealth. Those who do not have the initial resources (who you know) to use free enterprise also know that an imbalance of secondary sources (what is available to you). This relative victimization occurs through regulation which more often than not is enforced through government intervention.

In a government run by the people for the people, it is the people that raise these issue as they encounter them. The person in a lower class feels as though their relative victimization comes by way of deregulation which itself is also enforced through government intervention. The everchanging line of the ideal eustasis relies on the people to verbalize and make it so. Each person/group/party carries its own white flag including the government as is filibusters and lame ducks its way along in a political dance with its partners.

White flags(relative political correctness) is when each individuals feel as though they have been wronged or have been offended in some way so there is a flurry and a rush to raise their flag of offense regardless of how minute or flagrant the issue may be. The intention and theatrics involved with the flurry and the observed impression made by those raising the flag are what is used to justify the subjective objection, this is what we aptly name protesting, petitioning, standing your ground, and victimization. The prior stated are all subjective/emotional attempts to resolve and coalses objectiveness/reason.

The loud talking person who flails in relation to their government aid, which they have done nothing to earn and also the millionaire and billionaire who cries broke to the government are one in the same (which will be covered more thoroughly in the coming color/shades of America and her flag). This ping pong effect occurs daily and it varies in form and socio economic status. The true and good, purity of America, is the white flag of peace (of mind) that she has since her inception eternally swaddled in her additional colors or red and the following blue.

~Without conflict, there is no peace,
without peace there, is no conflict

Blue the color of the ethereal (heaven and earth)

Blue the color of serenity

Blue the color of intelligence

- My brothers in Blue aka the Thin blue line

To the service members whom I served with, I have faith in their training as a military force. I ponder with every new death if they are being trained as a policing force as they reintegrate into civilian arenas versus a secondary or toned down (more immersersed) military conduit when addressing the civilian population.when we allow our police force to become more immersed in the community we allow them to become more acute and surgical in their reactions within those arenas. After speaking with a number of servicemen active and within the police force as well, they have expressed that they desire for more in depth social interactions between them and the communities they police. They feel as though it will keep them safer as well as integrate a sensitive trust between them and their communities. Much like aiming for the hearts and minds. That was a military experiment attempted in a region that opposes the fabric of america and still made progress, with minimal comparative effort exponential progress may be had within the United States.

    We as a country are better because of our boys and girls in blue and also in spite of a minute fraction of them. We are better than the dismal excuse for policing that equates to tacky conflict, and at times the lack of justice/peace that constitutionally follows in declaration. We have been blessed to be born in and indoctrinated into a country that boast its blue ribbon training and lifestyle that affords the blue skies hang over the american dream.

~Pale Blue Dot- A increasing carbon footprint - we as a species are now temporarily relegated to residing on this planet. This small planet hanging in the midst of a vast universe has encapsulated all life that we know and have known and experienced as a species, even with the interaction and intervention of the all divine, God, or Gods depending upon your belief. We are slowly depleting the resource that have allowed us to flourish up till this very breath and moment. As we realize it will not be our government(a group of individuals) who saves the world but the actions of Every individual in realizing that earth is like a parent in hospice due to abuse and violence at the hand of her very own children.

We must pause and adjust our actions to reflect the care and appreciation that is required, so that we may understand the ways in which earth will need assistance to regaining more of her natural functions back, as the surf and turf change.

Let us as Americans lead the way in the creation of a better earth, better lifestyle, more jobs, durable infrastructure coupled by industry and arts as a reflection there of. Creating a strength through this diversification will be reflected in our global portfolio. It is our responsibility to think globally and act locally to ensure the betterment of our lives on this Pale Blue Dot.

www.ingramcontent.com/pod-product-compliance
Lightning Source LLC
Chambersburg PA
CBHW081022240526
45471CB00018B/3947